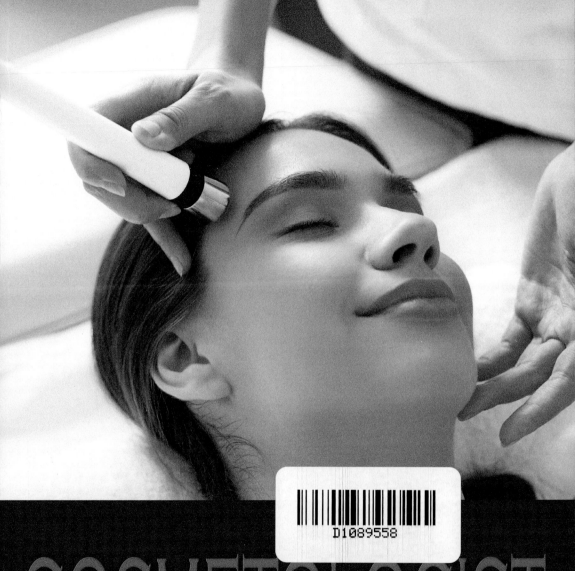

D1089558

COSMETOLOGIST

BRING BEAUTY TO YOUR CLIENT

CAREERS WITH EARNING POTENTIAL

CAR MECHANIC

CHEF

COSMETOLOGIST

DOG GROOMER

MASSAGE THERAPIST

FARMER

THE ARTS

PRESENTING YOURSELF

CAREERS WITH EARNING POTENTIAL

COSMETOLOGIST
BRING BEAUTY TO YOUR CLIENT

Christie Marlowe and Andrew Morkes

MASON CREST
PHILADELPHIA
MIAMI

Mason Crest
450 Parkway Drive, Suite D
Broomall, Pennsylvania 19008
(866) MCP-BOOK (toll-free)
www.masoncrest.com

First printing
9 8 7 6 5 4 3 2 1

ISBN (hardback) 978-1-4222-4324-4
ISBN (series) 978-1-4222-4319-0
ISBN (ebook) 978-1-4222-7488-0

Cataloging in Publication Data on file with the publisher.

Developed and Produced by National Highlights, Inc.
Editor: Andrew Gance
Interior and cover design: Jana Rade, impact studios
Interior layout: Tara Raymo, CreativelyTara
Production: Michelle Luke
Proofreader: Abby Jaworski

TABLE OF CONTENTS

KEY ICONS TO LOOK FOR:

WORDS TO UNDERSTAND: These words with their easy-to-understand definitions will increase the reader's understanding of the text while building vocabulary skills.

SIDEBARS: This boxed material within the main text allows readers to build knowledge, gain insights, explore possibilities, and broaden their perspectives by weaving together additional information to provide realistic and holistic perspectives.

EDUCATIONAL VIDEOS: Readers can view videos by scanning our QR codes, providing them with additional educational content to supplement the text. Examples include news coverage, moments in history, speeches, iconic sports moments, and much more!

TEXT-DEPENDENT QUESTIONS: These questions send the reader back to the text for more careful attention to the evidence presented there.

RESEARCH PROJECTS: Readers are pointed toward areas of further inquiry connected to each chapter. Suggestions are provided for projects that encourage deeper research and analysis.

SERIES GLOSSARY OF KEY TERMS: This back-of-the-book glossary contains terminology used throughout this series. Words found here increase the reader's ability to read and comprehend higher-level books and articles in this field.

WORDS TO UNDERSTAND

graduate degree: an educational credential that is awarded to someone who completes a master's degree or a PhD after getting a four-year bachelor's degree

industry: a particular area of business, such as car manufacturing or hospitality

salon: a business where beauty work is done

spa: a business that is focused on health, relaxation, and beauty treatments, including massages and facials

vocational: directed at a particular job

CHAPTER 1

THE ART OF MAKING PEOPLE LOOK GOOD

THE WORLD OF COSMETOLOGY

Cosmetologists have turned making people beautiful into a career. Using makeup, hair gel, scissors, and nail polish, cosmetologists spend their time helping people look their best. Cosmetologists include those who work with hair, skin, makeup, and nails. As a group, they are sometimes known as *personal appearance workers* and *beauty care professionals*. All cosmetologists work with physical appearance and use special techniques to make people look more beautiful.

But cosmetology is more than just giving makeovers and cutting hair. Karen Gordon, a cosmetologist who owns a **salon**, describes why she loves the field. "I always loved hair and fashion, and I love the service **industry**," she says.

More men are choosing to pursue careers in cosmetology.

(The service industry consists of all the businesses that do work, or that sometimes provide goods, for customers.) "There is an old saying that you give what you hope to get back in return," Karen explains. "I love making people look and feel better about themselves, and I love it when people make me feel that way too." Karen gets a lot of satisfaction from her job because she knows that she's helping people. People like to look beautiful, and she in turn feels good for helping her customers.

You'll find cosmetologists in salons and **spas**. You might even see them on TV, on the internet, and as the authors of books. You'll definitely see their work everywhere—fancy and cutting-edge hairstyles, manicures, and makeovers are all the work of personal appearance workers.

The women and men who choose cosmetology as a career know a lot. They understand exactly how to make anyone look their best. However, only a few cosmetologists learned their job in college. Instead, most of them took a different path.

DECIDING ON COLLEGE (OR NOT)

Choosing whether or not to attend college is a very big decision. Some young people know they want to go to college. Their families probably support their decision and may help them pay for it as well.

Other young people are ready to make money, not spend it on college, which can be very expensive. Many schools cost $40,000 or more a year. Although not all are quite that expensive, they may still cost too much for some families to afford. For other young people, college might not be the best place to get an education. Not everyone learns best in a classroom; many people would rather acquire knowledge by doing, not sitting in a class. And college does not provide the training for every job. If you want to be a mechanic, a plumber, or a cosmetologist, you don't need to go to college. You will definitely need to learn plenty of things to be good in these jobs—but you don't have to go to a four-year college to learn them.

You have lots of choices after high school. If a four-year college isn't right for you, maybe a technical school is. Technical schools are also called trade schools or **vocational** schools. At a technical school, students learn the skills and knowledge they need for a particular job. Students study for a year or two before they graduate, and then they can look for a job. Some schools even have job placement offices that help students get jobs. Trade schools teach all sorts of jobs, from hair styling to medical assisting to woodworking. Other jobs, however, require a four-year college degree (or even a **graduate degree**). Teachers and engineers, for example, have all earned at least a bachelor's degree in their fields.

Learn more about education and careers in cosmetology.

An apprentice observes a makeup artist at work.

Apprenticeships are another choice for people who don't want or need to go to college. Like technical schools, apprenticeships teach you how to do a specific job. Apprentices learn how to do the most basic things in their fields by working on the job. A cosmetology apprentice at a hair salon, for example, might learn how to wash customers' hair, clean the salon, and start to cut basic styles. The longer an apprentice works, the more they learn.

No matter what you decide—whether to go to college or take a different route—you'll have to be prepared to work hard. Not going to college after high school doesn't mean you have a free pass to be lazy! You'll still have lots to learn, and you will need to show that you are willing to work hard.

AN INSPIRING CAREER

Many cosmetologists knew they wanted to work with hair and makeup since they were young. Most did not go to college because they didn't need to. Instead, they learned how to be personal appearance professionals right away so they could start doing what they loved as soon as possible. Today, they can't imagine themselves doing anything else!

In an online article, celebrity makeup artist Carmindy tells the story of why she was inspired (the urge to do something out of the ordinary) to keep going with cosmetology. As a teenager, Carmindy worked at a Merle Norman makeup counter at the mall, giving people makeovers. She says, "One day I was standing at the Merle Norman counter, my brushes at the ready, my favorite lipsticks lined up. A woman with deep creases etched in her forehead came in. 'Do you think you could help me?' she asked hesitantly. 'I'd be glad to,' I said.

"She sank into the chair opposite me. 'I need a complete makeover,' she said. She had a pretty smile, but there was something so sad about her. She could

BEAUTY FIRSTS

3000 BCE: Nail polish and painted lipstick
1000 BCE (or earlier): Perfume
950 CE: Solid lipstick
1878 CE: Vaseline petroleum jelly
1890 CE: Electric hair dryer
1907 CE: Synthetic hair dye
1913 CE: Nontoxic mascara
1916 CE: Bobby pins
1923 CE: Cotton swabs
1930 CE: Lip gloss
1936 CE: Sunscreen
1948 CE: Hairspray

Sources: HistoryofCosmetics.net, Beautisecrets.com

hardly glance in the mirror before turning away, and I wondered what made her feel so unhappy with herself."

Carmindy began to do what she did best. "'Let's start with some foundation,' I said. I went through several to find just the right shade that would bring out her skin's glow. There's something very intimate [overly familiar or close] about putting makeup on someone. You're leaning close to her, touching her face. It feels natural to start chatting. And that's what I did with her, as I did with all my clients. I wanted to know something about them—where they lived, what they liked to do, how many children they had. If I saw a spark, I'd get a better idea of what made them tick. But there didn't seem to be anything this woman was passionate about.

"I swirled some blush on, and all at once tears started rolling down her cheeks. 'I'm so sorry,' I said, getting her a tissue. 'Are you okay? Was it something I did?' She shook her head. 'It's my husband,' she said. 'Nothing I do ever pleases him. He criticizes everything—my cooking, my clothes, my looks.'"

Carmindy continues with her story. "She talked some more and I listened while I worked, applying a sheer eye shadow, dabbing gloss on her lips. I didn't feel qualified to give her advice about marriage—I was just a teenager, after all—but I wanted to show her how lovely she was. Her smile was warm and her eyes, even when she was so upset, were soft and kind.

"For a while we were both silent, that silence of two people concentrating together. I did my best to make my work convey to her what my mother said to me, 'You're beautiful just as you are.' When I was finished, I turned her chair to face the mirror. And in that moment, she saw it. 'You've made me beautiful!' she exclaimed. 'No,' I said, 'I didn't do that. That's how you were made.'"

Carmindy at Daily Front Row's Fashion Media Awards.

Carmindy says that day, and others like them, convinced her she needed to be a cosmetologist. She wasn't sure where her path would lead next, but she knew she had to try. She loved helping women see how beautiful they were, and cosmetology was the right career.

Because of her passion (an intense feeling of excitement for something) and her dedication (being committed to a goal), Carmindy has become a successful makeup artist. She has worked with celebrities, she starred on TLC's *What Not to Wear* for ten years, and she has written several books. She is happy with her life as a beauty expert, just like she knew she would be as a teenager at the mall.

RESEARCH PROJECT

Talk to people who have trained for a career via an apprenticeship, in technical school, and by attending college. Ask them what they liked and disliked about their education. Consider their responses as you make the decision on whether to attend college or train for a career in another way. Based on your research and your own interests, what is the best educational path for you?

TEXT-DEPENDENT QUESTIONS

1. What do cosmetologists do?
2. What is a spa?
3. What inspired Carmindy to enter the field?

WORDS TO UNDERSTAND

consultation: a professional discussion with someone to get advice

dermatology: the study and treatment of skin disorders

exfoliate: to rub a part of the body to remove dead skin cells

hair extensions: pieces of artificial or natural hair that are added to make natural hair longer

CHAPTER 2

WHAT DO COSMETOLOGISTS DO?

COSMETOLOGY: A WORLD OF OPPORTUNITIES

There are more than 536,000 cosmetologists in the United States. Many millions more work throughout the world. Some cut and style hair. Others work with makeup. Still others give manicures and pedicures. Finally, some cosmetologists focus on skin care and skin treatments. All these personal appearance workers keep people looking beautiful.

If you're looking into cosmetology as a career, you have a lot of choices. You can explore different areas of beauty and decide which one is the best for you. The following section provides more information on career paths in cosmetology.

A career as a hair stylist is a good fit for those who are creative and like to work with their hands.

HAIRSTYLISTS

Hairstylists are the people who cut and style hair. Most people go to the stylist every few months or so. Hairstylists can change your style with a few snips or maybe some hair dye or highlights.

Stylists have to understand hair. They need to know how to cut both thick and thin hair. They can't just take scissors and chop away. Instead, they study the customer and figure out exactly what they want and what would look best. Then the hairstylist must do their best to make it happen.

Customers want a variety of things done to their hair. They want it trimmed or cut. They want it dyed, straightened, or curled. They want it washed and blow-dried perfectly. Some customers want **hair extensions**. A hairstylist needs to know how to do all those things.

Besides fashion and styling, hairstylists know about the structure and health of hair. They give customers advice on making hair healthier because they know what products to use and what hairstyling techniques or processes can damage the hair.

Some hairstylists specialize in certain kinds of customers. *Barbers* often cut men's hair. Other hairstylists work with women's hair, curly hair, or

Job opportunities are increasing for barbers as more men—especially those in their 20s—focus on their personal appearance.

BE PREPARED

Successful beauty professionals love their jobs, but not everything about their work is perfect. It's a good idea to get to know some of the downsides of cosmetology so you'll be prepared. For example, cosmetologists often stand for eight, nine, ten, or more hours every day. They get tired feet, shoulders, and backs. They need to take time to relax and move around. The long hours and work on evenings and weekends also tire people out. Customers can be demanding or simply rude. Personal appearance professionals sometimes get fed up with how much their jobs focus on physical appearance. However, cosmetologists who really love their profession focus on the great parts of the job, so they can deal with a bad day now and then.

African American hair. Each type of hairstylist has to know how to give customers what they need.

Other cosmetologists have specialized duties. *Colorists* are hairstylists who have been specially trained to apply color to a client's hair. They receive specialized training that can take several years. Colorists often work in the color department of a large salon. *Shampooers* are typically entry-level hairstylists who wash a customer's hair before it is cut by a more experienced stylist.

Karen Gordon focuses on cutting and styling hair. In an interview, she discusses her everyday duties. "Along with all of the day-to-day management responsibilities of running a successful salon," she says, "my responsibilities

Some hair stylists specialize in cutting certain types of hair, such as African American hair.

ARE MEN COSMETOLOGISTS?

Plenty of men are cosmetologists! About 90 percent of beauty care workers (BCWs) are women. In other words, nine out of ten cosmetologists are women. But that means 10 percent of the 536,000 BCWs are men—more than 53,000 of them to be exact. And more and more men are starting out in the field. Cosmetology schools report that numbers of male students are rising. There are even famous male cosmetologists—such as Mario Tricoci and John Frieda—with their own lines of beauty products.

as a hairdresser include providing a thorough and professional **consultation** with my clients, performing to the best of my abilities the services that we agree upon, and recommending proper techniques and products so that my clients can maintain their style/color at home."

She goes on to say, "It is also my responsibility to provide a clean and safe environment for my clients and coworkers, and to complete continuing education about the latest trends and technologies [equipment or software that is created to do specific tasks] for my industry. I usually see a client every forty-five minutes, or every hour if they require more complicated services. I don't take a lunch break, and I prefer to eat when I am between clients. That's pretty normal for a hairdresser!"

Karen is happy working with her customers. She explains, "I suppose that it would be fun to be a hairdresser backstage at fashion shows and hang out with models and celebrities. But if I had really wanted to do that, I would have gone out and done that years ago." Her busy schedule keeps her working hard, but it's work she finds worthwhile.

A makeup artist needs to enjoy bringing out the best in others' appearance.

MAKEUP ARTISTS

Other cosmetologists work mostly with makeup. Lots of *makeup artists* work with ordinary people who want to add some glamour (extreme attractiveness and a celebrity-like look) to their lives. They give women makeovers and apply makeup for special events such as weddings. These makeup artists listen to customers and figure out what they want. They know which colors of makeup work best with different skin tones, and how to work with all kinds of makeup, such as eyeliner, foundation, and mascara.

Other makeup artists work with actors, models, and other celebrities. Film studios use makeup artists to give actors the right look for their roles. *Special-effects makeup artists* know how to turn actors into animals, monsters, or older or younger versions of themselves using makeup techniques. TV stations also hire makeup artists to work with newscasters and talk show hosts.

ESTHETICIANS

Cosmetologists who deal with skin care work in esthetics. *Estheticians*, as they're known, help customers take care of their skin.

Estheticians, who are also known as *skin care specialists*, are trained in several different skin care techniques. They can give customers facials, **exfoliate** their skin, or remove unwanted hair.

Although most estheticians aren't medical professionals, they sometimes work with doctors. If an esthetician sees something wrong with a customer's skin, they can recommend the customer go see a doctor. Estheticians should be able to spot things that might need a doctor's attention.

Some professionals are actually *medical estheticians*. They have had more training in medical knowledge about skin. Medical estheticians work in **dermatology** offices or plastic surgery offices.

COSMETIC PRODUCT CATEGORIES

- Baby products
- Bath preparations
- Eye makeup preparations
- Fragrance preparations
- Hair preparations (non-coloring)
- Hair coloring preparations
- Makeup preparations
- Manicuring preparations
- Oral hygiene products
- Personal cleanliness products
- Shaving preparations
- Skin care preparations
- Suntan preparations

Source: U.S. Food & Drug Administration

NAIL PROFESSIONALS

Nail professionals focus on nails. They clean, trim, and polish fingernails and toenails. They also know how to work with fake nails. Some nail professionals are artists, creating pictures, designs, and patterns on the tiny surfaces of nails. Many also know how to massage hands and feet, and make the skin on hands and feet healthier and beautiful.

Nail professionals work in a salon where other beauty treatments are available, or they work in nail salons that are entirely dedicated to nail care. *Manicurists* are nail professionals who specialize in providing cosmetic treatments to the nails and hands. *Pedicurists* focus on the feet. Many nail professionals work on both the hands and feet.

Nail technicians must be comfortable touching people's hands and feet.

DAILY LIFE

The good thing about cosmetology is that you have a lot of room to decide how you want to organize your schedule. Some personal appearance professionals work part time. They have another job or they take care of their children at home. They might work twenty hours a week, or a little more or a little less.

Other cosmetologists own their own businesses. Karen, for example, owns her salon with her husband and has hired more than twenty other people to work for her. Owning a business is a lot of work. Salon owners often work more than forty hours a week. They work in the evenings and sometimes six or seven days a week, depending on how many customers they want to have. There's always something to be done if you're a busy owner.

Personal appearance professionals work at a variety of places. Many work in a salon or spa with other cosmetologists. There may be anywhere from two to dozens of cosmetologists all working in the same space. Others work at home or in businesses they own themselves. Customers come to their homes to get their hair cut or makeup done. Sometimes hairstylists or makeup artists will even travel to the homes of their customers. These professionals can make their

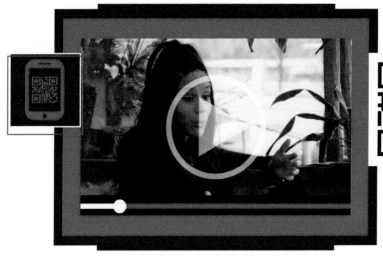

A hair salon owner discusses why she entered the field and the rewards and challenges of her work.

own schedules since they work for themselves. Smaller numbers of beauty care professionals work at hotels, resorts, and spas, as well as on cruise ships.

All cosmetologists have some things in common. Salons and spas are businesses and have to be run professionally. Beauty care professionals must keep their workspaces clean, including their tools. Unclean combs, scissors, and makeup brushes can spread diseases, so cosmetologists have to be

U.S. SPA FACTS, 2017

- The spa industry generated more than $17.5 billion in revenue, up from $9.7 billion in revenue in 2005.
- There were 187 million spa visits.
- Approximately 372,100 people worked in the spa industry.
- There were 21,770 spas.

Source: International Spa Association

extra careful. Many cosmetologists also have to schedule appointments, keep track of customer records, and use cash registers for payments. Helping run the business is part of being a beauty care professional.

YOUR FIRST JOB

Your first job might not be the most glamorous or the best paying. Once you get your license (permission given by a government agency to work in a particular field), you'll have to decide what to do next. You'll have to be patient and persistent (continuing to work hard despite challenges). Finding a job might take a few weeks or even a few months. Apply to lots of places, and keep an open mind. Be confident when you interview. You might even have to prove you know what you're doing in an interview by actually showing your skills on a customer or on a friend you bring with you.

Your first job might turn out to be working as an assistant or an apprentice. Be positive, and you'll learn a lot. Work hard. Instead of grumbling while you clean floors and do laundry, watch what your coworkers are doing. Be respectful, and offer to help when needed. Once your boss knows you are friendly and a hard worker, you might have opportunities to move up.

There are many employment options for cosmetologists, including owning a salon.

When you start working with clients, try your hardest. Be friendly, listen to what your client wants, and do your best work. If your client is happy, they will come back again and again to see you. Try to stick with one job for a while. Even if you don't think it's perfect, keep the job for a bit. You might end up liking it a lot more. And staying with one job helps you build up clients who know you and want you to cut their hair or do their makeup. When you're ready to move to a different job, some of your clients will come with you.

Don't get frustrated that you don't know everything right away. Cosmetologists work for years to build their skills. You just have to be patient— and one day, you'll be styling hair, painting nails, or applying lipstick with the best of them.

YOUR FUTURE IN COSMETOLOGY

After you spend some time at your first job, you'll have learned all sorts of new skills and met lots of new people. What's next?

You have a few choices. You could look for a job working in a fancier salon that charges more and is known for good work—and probably pays better too. You could start your own business out of your home, or start your own salon. Owning a business means you have more control over your job and you will make more money. You could also work as a teacher at a beauty school, start looking for work as a celebrity cosmetologist, or start your own line of beauty products.

If you think cosmetology might be for you, start learning now! As Karen the salon owner says, "I love my work and I love my clients. Surveys show that hairstylists are among the most professionally satisfied people."

What more could you ask for in life?

Once you land a job, it's important to work hard and always have a great attitude.

RESEARCH PROJECT

Create a list of cosmetology careers that you're interested in (e.g., hairstylist, skin care specialist, manicurist, etc.). Learn what the educational requirements and job duties are for each career. Then create a list of pluses and minuses for each occupation. This will help you decide which is the best fit for your interests and educational goals.

TEXT-DEPENDENT QUESTIONS

1. What is a hair extension?
2. What do makeup artists do?
3. What are some of the challenges of working as a cosmetologist?

CHAPTER 3

TERMS OF THE TRADE

acetone: A chemical solvent that is used to dissolve nail polish and acrylics for removal.

acrylic brush: A special brush with natural hair bristles that is used to apply acrylic nail product.

acrylic nails: Artificial nails; people often get them if they want a different-shaped nail or a longer nail.

airbrushing: The process of using an airbrush gun to create a nail design or to apply makeup.

bangs: The strands of hair cut to cover the forehead; also known as **fringe** in the United Kingdom.

blow-dryer: An electric-powered device that is used to dry a customer's hair.

blush: A powder or cream cosmetic that is used to color the cheeks in varying shades. It is also known as **rouge**.

body: The volume of a person's hair.

buffer: A beauty tool with rigid gritty surfaces that is used to give fingernails and toenails a high-gloss shine.

chemical cut: Hair that is so over-processed (with bleaches, dyes, and straighteners) that it breaks and looks as though it has been cut.

color depth: The darkness or lightness of hair color.

conditioner: A hair care product that is applied to allow easier brushing or combing of the hair and improve its feel and appearance.

curling iron: A heated, rod-shaped tool that is used to curl hair.

dermatology: The study and treatment of skin disorders.

diffuser: An attachment to a hair dryer that is used to spread out its airflow. Diffusers are used primarily for people with curly hair.

drying lamp: Equipment that is used to dry nails after they have been painted.

dusting: A haircutting technique in which the stylist removes just enough hair to freshen the ends.

elasticity: The degree to which hair can be stretched and return to its original shape.

exfoliate: To rub a part of the body to remove dead skin cells.

eye shadow: A cosmetic (typically powder) that is applied on the eyelids and under the eyebrows in order to make the wearer's eyes stand out and look more attractive.

eyeliner: A cosmetic that is used to apply color to the area around the eyes to emphasize and highlight their appearance.

facial: A skin treatment that cleans the pores (tiny openings in the skin), exfoliates away dead skin cells, and treats common skin issues. The goal of a facial is to make the skin look healthier and younger and provide a relaxing experience to the client.

flat iron: A heated tool that is used to flatten or otherwise style hair.

foundation: A cream, liquid, or powder that is applied to the face to create an even, uniform color to the complexion. It is also used to cover scars or blemishes, to change the natural skin tone, and as a moisturizer, sunscreen, astringent (a chemical that is used to minimize pores and dry up oily skin), or a base layer for more complex cosmetics.

hair extensions: Pieces of artificial or natural hair that are added to make natural hair longer.

hair highlighting: The process of changing a person's hair color by adding color that is lighter than their hair.

hair lowlighting: The process of changing a person's hair color by adding color that is darker than their hair.

hair roller: A small tube that is rolled into a client's hair to curl or straighten it; also known as a **hair curler**.

hair styling station: The main work area for a hairstylist. It contains a mirror, tool holders, tool compartment, storage drawers, customer chair, and an electrical outlet.

highlights: The color in specific sections of a person's hair.

layers: A haircutting technique that results in different lengths of hair at the ends, with the goal of decreasing the density of hair and giving the hair a sense of movement.

makeover: The complete change of a person's hairstyle, makeup, clothing, and other areas of appearance.

manicure: The cosmetic treatments of the nails and hands.

mascara: A cosmetic that is used to thicken and darken the eyelashes.

massage: The rubbing and kneading of soft body tissues (muscle, connective tissue, ligaments, and tendons) to improve a person's health and promote relaxation.

nail file: A tool that is used to smooth and shape the fingernails and toenails.

nail polish: A lacquer that is applied to fingernails or toenails to make them more attractive and protect the nail plates.

nipper: A nail tool with multiple uses, including cuticle care, nail clipping, and acrylic nipping.

pedicure: The cosmetic treatment of the toenails and feet.

pedicure chair: A chair, often with a built-in foot bath, that the client sits in during a pedicure.

perm: A type of hairstyle in which heat and chemicals are applied to give the hair a long-lasting curl or wave. It is also known as a **permanent wave**.

relaxer: A chemical method that is used to straighten hair.

salon: A store where beauty work is done.

sanitation station: An area of a salon or spa where combs, nail equipment and other cosmetology tools are sanitized.

scissors: A hand tool that is used to cut hair.

sectioning: The process of dividing hair into smaller sections to cut, style, or dry one area at a time.

shampoo bowl: A type of sink that is used to wash a client's hair before styling

shears: A haircutting tool that is significantly sharper than an average pair of scissors. They are typically 5 to 7 inches (12.7 to 17.8 centimeters) long and have a hook, known as a finger brace, attached to one of the finger rings that allows the stylist to maintain better control while cutting.

spa: A business that is focused on health, relaxation, and beauty treatment including massages, steam baths, and exercise.

stencil: A guide that is used when creating nail art. They are commonly used in airbrushing nail art techniques.

stippling brush: A brush that is used to apply foundation, powder, blush bronzer, and highlighters in a dot form. Using a stippling brush allows the makeup artist to create a smoother, more diffused finish as opposed to rubbing the face with a stiff brush.

straight razor: A long sharp blade that is set in a handle that folds open and closed; it is used to shave a man's facial hair.

texturizing: The process of giving a blunt or pure form shape in order to create different lengths and movement in a client's hair.

thinning: A haircutting technique that uses texturizing shears to reduce the thickness of hair.

undercutting: A haircutting technique that is done to prevent the hair at the back of the head from growing longer than the rest of the hair as it grows.

WORDS TO UNDERSTAND

anatomy: the study of the human body

chain: a business with at least two, but often many, units

cosmetic counter: a store area where all the products of a makeup line are displayed; a salesperson demonstrates the positive effects on a potential customer to encourage a purchase

perks: the benefits or advantages to having a particular job

CHAPTER 4

PREPARING FOR THE FIELD AND MAKING A LIVING

BECOMING A COSMETOLOGIST

You won't need to go to college to train to be a cosmetologist. However, you'll still need to learn a lot before you can start cutting hair, painting nails, or giving makeovers.

Carmindy describes her rise to the top of the cosmetologist world. "When I was fifteen years old I became obsessed with makeup and began practicing on myself and friends. I would tear out pictures from magazines, read every book out there about fashion and dream big, picturing myself traveling the world

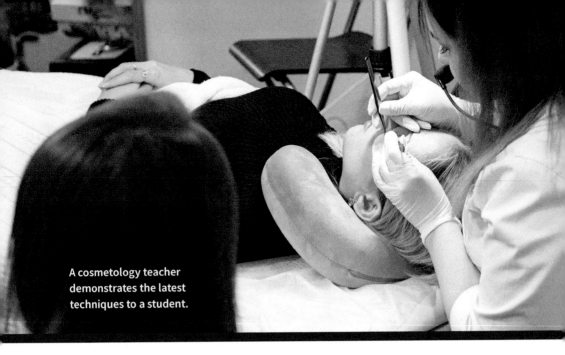

A cosmetology teacher demonstrates the latest techniques to a student.

over, painting faces. One day I discovered that my friend's father was a makeup artist for a TV show in Hollywood. I would go over to his house and question him for hours about the industry, checking out his makeup and toolbox and learning about how to break into the biz. There was no real industry then and I had to do a lot of digging to find out how to become a makeup artist." Carmindy started with passion, and then figured out whether she could turn that passion into a career.

As it turned out, Carmindy definitely *could* make a career out of makeup. She got some more early experience. "I kept practicing doing makeup on friends," she says, "and when I was seventeen I got a job working at a **cosmetic counter** at the mall. I then signed up at a hair and makeup agency as an apprentice and for two years worked on set assisting. I cleaned brushes, fetched coffee, organized lipsticks, and watched, listened, and learned." At seventeen, Carmindy also started taking makeup classes. "I took a few courses in Los Angeles from a makeup artist named Maurice Stein. He owned a makeup company and school called Cinema Secrets. This was a man I wanted to impress with my talent because he was so seasoned [experienced and knowledgeable] and a great teacher. When he always seemed to give me the highest score in the class I knew I was on the right path."

Then Carmindy got a big opportunity. She had earned a reputation as a hard worker on fashion sets. She says, "The photographer's assistants would ask me if I wanted to do test shooting over the weekend with new models and I would do it for free to build my portfolio. [A portfolio is a collection of one's work organized for other people to see.] One magic day the professional makeup artist I was assisting became ill and I had to step in and do a swimwear catalog and the photographer liked my work better and that was the beginning of my career."

From there, Carmindy took every opportunity she could. Eventually, she started traveling to do fashion shoots around the country. And then the creators of the TV show *What Not to Wear* noticed her. She became the makeover artist

Learn about a cosmetology training program for high school students.

on the show, started her own line of beauty products, and began writing books. Now she is one of the most famous makeup artists around.

Not everyone's path will be exactly like Carmindy's. Most cosmetologists don't become famous as TV stars. But they do share some things with Carmindy—the willingness to work hard and a love of the job.

EARLY EXPERIENCE

Many future cosmetologists realize they want to work with hair, makeup, nails, and skin early on. They discover they like to cut their own hair, or they give friends beauty advice. Like Carmindy, some young people start experimenting on themselves and friends.

Sometimes high schools offer vocational classes where students can explore future careers. If you think you might be interested in cosmetology, you can ask around to see if your school has one of these programs. Then you can take a class or two in hairstyling, skin care, or makeup application and see what you think. If you don't like your classes, then you know the field of personal appearance might not be for you. If you do like them, you'll know you want to keep learning cosmetology and maybe make a career out of it.

If you take a cosmetology class at a trade school, you will probably practice on mannequins before working with actual people.

COSMETOLOGY SCHOLARSHIPS

The Beauty Changes Lives foundation was founded to support the next generation of beauty and wellness professionals. Since its creation, it has awarded more than $2 million in scholarships to cosmetology, nail, massage, and esthetic students. Applicants must be accepted to or attending a cosmetology school. Scholarship awards range from $1,000 to $15,000. Visit https://beautychangeslives.org to learn more.

Even if your school doesn't have a cosmetology program, you'll still need to finish high school and earn a diploma. Many beauty care positions require you to have a high school diploma. For people who don't graduate, a GED is usually ok instead of a high school diploma. GED stands for general equivalency diploma. If a person does not graduate from high school, they can later study and take the GED tests. Passing the GED tests is equivalent to getting a high school diploma.

COSMETOLOGY SCHOOL

Cosmetology school is one of the best places to learn how to be a hairstylist, barber, or makeup artist. At the end, you'll get a degree or a certificate (an educational credential that usually takes about a year to earn) that prepares you to start working as a beauty care professional.

Some cosmetology programs are more general, and students learn about hairstyling, nail care, skin care, and other fields. Others let students pick one kind of cosmetology to study and get really good at that one thing.

Students may take courses in haircutting and styling, hair coloring, manicures and pedicures, facials, makeup, and more. Some students, such as those studying esthetics, also take science courses like chemistry and **anatomy**. Other classes might include salon management and business math.

You'll get experience actually doing hair, makeup, and nails while you're in cosmetology school. Many programs have a salon where customers can come in for a low price, or even for free. Customers get haircuts, makeup, and manicures done by cosmetology students. School salons are a good way for students to practice with real-life clients before they start a job.

Cosmetology programs cost less than college, but they can still be expensive depending on where you go. The average cost of cosmetology school in the United States is between $10,000 and $20,000. Specific programs focused on makeup artistry or esthetics are often less expensive, though. They can cost between $3,000 and $5,000. You'll also need to buy your own books and supplies, like scissors, makeup, and aprons.

You might be able to get financial aid such as student loans or scholarships. Student loans supply money that students borrow for school and must pay back after graduation. A scholarship is money given to a student to help pay for school. They do not have to pay the money back. Students who need money or who are very good at academics or sports sometimes receive scholarships. Schools know that not everyone can afford $20,000, so they give money to many students. Beauty associations and government agencies also provide loans, scholarships, and other types of financial aid.

Cosmetology school takes anywhere from nine months to a couple of years to finish. However, shorter programs don't always give you enough training. You want to find a program that gives you enough support to really learn new skills. You don't want to graduate and realize you can't get a job anywhere because you don't know enough!

Look around for a cosmetology school that is right for you. If you want to focus on nail care, make sure the schools you're applying to offer training in nail care. If you can't afford an expensive school, look around for cheaper schools that will still give you the skills you need. Go visit the school and talk to the students and teachers. Are students happy there? Do the students who graduate get good jobs right away? Ask questions so you know what you're getting yourself into. You should also check out reviews of the school that people post on social media.

Accreditation

Make sure that you attend a school that is accredited. An accredited cosmetology school has met minimum standards that have been set by a governing organization. By attending an accredited school, you'll be sure to receive a quality education that will prepare you for a career in cosmetology. In the United States, the National Accrediting Commission of Career Arts & Sciences accredits

Learn five things you should consider before enrolling in a beauty school.

WHAT WILL I ACTUALLY LEARN?

Many cosmetology schools teach the topics covered by one textbook in particular, called *Milady's Standard Cosmetology*. The topics covered include the following:

- basic life skills (such as setting goals and maintaining a positive attitude)
- developing a professional image
- communication skills
- infection control (including how to prevent the spread of hepatitis, HIV, or other infectious viruses or bacteria in a salon)
- general anatomy and physiology
- basics of chemistry and electricity
- hair and scalp characteristics
- principles of hair design (such as how to enhance a person's look based on facial shape)
- basic hair care (shampooing, rinsing, and conditioning)
- basic haircutting (including core cuts)
- hairstyling (including how to use the proper tools and techniques)
- hair braiding and braid extensions
- hair coloring
- chemical hair texturing
- wigs and other hair enhancements
- properties of skin and nails (including how they grow)
- skin diseases and disorders
- hair removal (such as waxing and tweezing)
- performing basic facials
- makeup
- nail diseases and disorders
- performing manicures
- performing pedicures
- creating a résumé and portfolio
- preparing for job interviews
- basic business skills
- preparing for state licensure exams

cosmetology schools. You can search for accredited schools at http://naccas. org/naccas/accredited-school-search. There are accrediting agencies in other countries too. If you don't live in the United States, check with your country's department of professional regulation for more information.

APPRENTICESHIPS

Aspiring cosmetologists have the choice of participating in an apprenticeship before they get a full-time job. Apprenticeships offer a combination of classroom and on-the-job training. They also can last longer than cosmetology school. Some people get most of their training through an apprenticeship and not a cosmetology school. Check with your state's department of professional regulation to see if you're allowed to do that.

A makeup apprentice at work.

You also may be able to participate in an apprenticeship after cosmetology school. That's what Karen Gordon did. She first went to cosmetology school to learn the basics. Then she got an apprenticeship at a salon so she could learn even more.

"After I graduated from cosmetology school, I worked as an apprentice for a year so that I could improve my skills," she explains. "I did shampooing, sweeping the floors, etc. It was hard work, but I learned a lot."

Karen advises new cosmetologists to do what she did. "When you get out of cosmetology school, become an apprentice in a great salon," she says. "Cosmetology school teaches you the basics. Take another year and invest in your career. Love what you do, and the money will come." After she finished her apprenticeship, Karen went on to co-own her own salon. Cosmetology school and the apprenticeship paid off!

LICENSING

Even after all that training, cosmetologists need to take one more step before they can work—they need to get licensed. A license is a document from the government that says a person can legally practice in a field, such as cosmetology. The government doesn't want people working who don't know what they're doing because cosmetology often involves health issues. For example, if a manicurist doesn't really know how to cut cuticles right, they may cause a customer's nails to get infected.

To get a license, you usually have to have a high school diploma (or a GED), be at least sixteen, and have graduated from a cosmetology school. Every state has different licensing rules, so check with your state before you make any decisions about how to learn cosmetology. Some states let you get a license after you finish an apprenticeship rather than cosmetology school.

You also need to take a test to get your license. The test has a written part and sometimes a second part where you will need to show your actual skills. You'll have to answer questions about sanitation (cleanliness), safety, chemicals used in cosmetology, skin care, salon management, and more. If you have worked hard at learning what you need to know, you'll pass the test.

Once you pass your exam, you'll need to get your license renewed every few years. If you move to another state, you might need to get a new license too. Most states don't accept licenses from other states.

HOW MUCH CAN I MAKE?

Hardworking cosmetologists can expect to make a good living. They may not be rich or famous, but they'll get paid for doing what they love. Cosmetologists are usually paid by the hour. Hairdressers, hairstylists, and cosmetologists earn $11.95 an hour, according to the U.S. Department of Labor (USDL). As a yearly income, that works out to be nearly $25,000, working forty hours a week all year long.

In reality, cosmetologists make all different amounts of money. A cosmetologist just starting out might make $8.73 an hour. They don't have much practice yet, and they won't have built up enough customers who come back again and again. The longer they stick with their job, though, the more money they'll make. Cosmetologists who choose to work part time may also make less per year because they are only working ten, twenty, or thirty hours a week. A cosmetologist who works twenty hours a week for $8.73 an hour will make about $9,000 over a whole year. That's not a lot of money.

Older cosmetologists who have been working for a while might make a lot more than $8.73 an hour. They are very skilled and have a lot of customers. They have clients who know them and love their work. They may own a salon, like Karen, and make a lot more money. The top 10 percent of cosmetologists make $41,500 or more. At the higher end, the most experienced cosmetologists can make $50,000 a year, including tips and bonuses.

Personal appearance workers make different amounts of money depending on where they work too. For example, a makeup artist who works in a big city will earn a lot more than a makeup artist who works in a tiny town. Some cities have established a minimum wage, the lowest amount someone can be paid. For example, the minimum wage in Seattle, Washington, is $15 an hour, so the

Barbers earn salaries that range from $18,000 to $48,000 or more, according to the USDL.

SALARIES FOR COSMETOLOGISTS BY U.S. STATE

Earnings for hairstylists and other types of cosmetologists vary by state based on demand and other factors. Here are the five states where employers pay the highest average salary and the states in which employers pay the lowest salaries.

Highest Average Salaries:	Lowest Average Salaries:
1. Washington: $40,680	1. South Carolina: $21,750
2. New Jersey: $37,660	2. Utah: $23,820
3. Massachusetts: $37,410	3. Louisiana: $24,130
4. Virginia: $37,070	4. Alabama: $24,190
5. Delaware: $35,340	5. New Mexico: $24,470

Source: USDL

lowest amount a full-time, salaried cosmetologist could earn would be $31,200. Of course, living in a big city is more expensive, and the cosmetologist will have to spend more money on housing, food, and other things.

SALARIES FOR OTHER BEAUTY PROFESSIONALS

The following paragraphs provide information on earnings for other types of beauty professionals, according to the USDL.

Skin care specialists earn median salaries of $30,080. Earnings range from $18,650 to $58,810.

The least-experienced and -skilled manicurists and pedicurists earn $19,480 a year. Those with a lot of experience and a large client base earn $33,050. The average manicurist or pedicurist earns $24,980 a year.

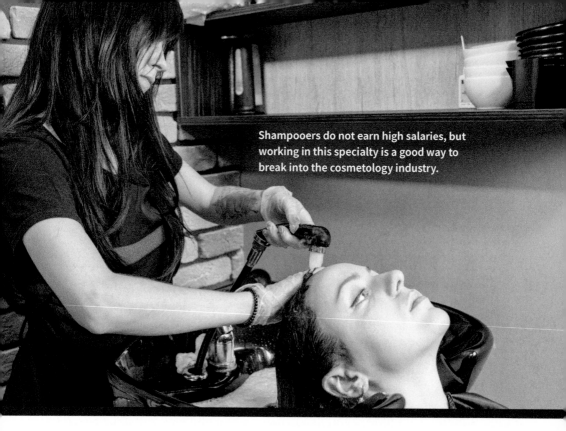

Shampooers do not earn high salaries, but working in this specialty is a good way to break into the cosmetology industry.

Shampooers earn median annual salaries of $20,320. Ten percent of shampooers earn $17,770, while the top 10 percent earn $27,040.

TIPS AND BONUSES

The USDL averages do not include tips. For each haircut, manicure, or makeover, a cosmetologist usually gets a tip from the customer. How much the tip is depends on where the cosmetologist works. A hairstylist at a **chain** salon might make $5 or $10 as a tip, but stylists at fancier salons may make 15 to 20 percent of the entire cost of the procedure. So if a haircut costs $100, the stylist might be tipped $15 to $20. But tipping is not "set in stone." It's important to remember that tipping varies greatly by the type of procedure, geographic area, and type of beauty facility.

Successful cosmetologists might also get bonuses (cash awards) from the salons where they work. Salons give out bonuses for bringing in a lot of new customers or selling a lot of beauty products.

BENEFITS

Benefits are extra things you get from an employer, such as health-care insurance and paid vacation days. Some salons offer benefits, but a lot don't. Look around for a job that gives you health insurance, paid vacation days, and overtime pay (a higher salary if you work additional hours). Benefits can be hard to find, though, so you might need to be willing to work for a few years without them until you have more experience.

STAR COSMETOLOGISTS

Some young cosmetologists dream about becoming rich and famous. If you're one of them, you'll need to work hard, meet new people, and have a little luck. But anything is possible!

Celebrity beauty care workers have some things in common. They are really good at what they do, for one. They have practiced for years, and they have perfected their techniques. They're also really passionate about their work. They love what they do, and they do it all the time. They knew they had to meet the right people and convince them they were amazing cosmetologists, so they also have a lot of confidence in themselves.

Some beauty care professionals work with movie or TV stars. You can find their hair and makeup work on screens around the world. Others work on fashion shoots for magazines or advertisements. A few even work for fashion

A FEW FAMOUS COSMETOLOGISTS

- Madam C.J. Walker (Sarah Breedlove) was the first African American to make hair care products, and the first African American woman to become a millionaire. She was born in 1867. She created a line of hair care products for scalp health and taught other black women how to take care of their hair. She worked for black rights.
- John Frieda is a British celebrity hairstylist. He started a line of hair products that are sold all over the world.
- Sally Hershberger is a hairstylist who is well known for creating Meg Ryan's famous haircut in the 1990s. She has also appeared on TV shows like *Shear Genius* and *America's Next Top Model*. Her haircuts are expensive—she used to charge $600 a haircut, and they're even more expensive today!
- Paul Mitchell was a Scottish hairstylist. He ran several famous salons and eventually started his own line of products. Mitchell's son is also a famous stylist.
- Vidal Sassoon was a British hairstylist who made a big name for himself starting in the 1960s. He first created a famous short haircut and then went on to start a line of hair care products that are still sold today.

shows, doing the hair and makeup for models. These individuals make more money than the average cosmetologist.

Beauty care professionals who work in the entertainment industry are paid quite well. Theatrical and performance makeup artists earn median annual salaries of $59,300 according to the USDL, while those who work in the motion picture and video industries earn $75,160. Earnings range from $21,250 to $127,030.

Some cosmetologists make money a different way. They start their own beauty product lines, which bring in extra money. Or they write a book about beauty advice, which also makes money. Cosmetologists may be on TV shows and on the internet. All of these kinds of cosmetologists become stars themselves!

Makeup artists who work in the fashion industry earn higher salaries than those who are employed at salons.

MONEY AND MORE

Those who work in the best jobs earn a good living. These jobs are also fun and help you learn new things and feel fulfilled (someone who is fulfilled is completely content with what they are doing). Cosmetologists love their jobs because of the people they meet, and because they love being creative with nail polish, makeup, scissors, and more.

Take Carmindy. She was on the TV show *What Not to Wear* for ten years, has her own line of beauty products, writes books, and gives interviews. You might think her favorite part of her job is the fame and fortune. However, Carmindy says otherwise. Even at a young age, Carmindy loved doing makeovers, and she wasn't very interested in the money she could get by doing them. As a teenager working at a Merle Norman counter at the mall, she had to sell makeup as part of her job. However, she says, "You know how I said I was more interested in the women themselves than in selling them Merle Norman products? Well, I got fired for not selling enough." She didn't care enough about the extra money she would get if she sold makeup—she just wanted to work with people and make them beautiful.

She goes on to say, "I promptly got a job doing makeovers at another place in the mall. I moved on from there, working with women all over the world (some models, some not), and eventually established myself as a top makeup artist. Today, I write books on beauty [her latest is *Bloom: A Girl's Guide to Growing Up Gorgeous*]. I've co-created a line of cosmetics." Her love of makeup and working with women of all types led to her fame and her money. The fame and money are great, but they wouldn't be worth it if Carmindy didn't love her job.

Carmindy explains some of the **perks** of her job today. "Being a makeup artist is wonderful. There is no better job in the world than making women feel and look incredible. Our entire society has us feeling insecure about ourselves and if you can make just one woman feel gorgeous and happy it is all worth it. Not to mention the new and interesting people you get to meet, the exotic traveling you get to do, and also the escape from a regular 9-to-5 [job], which is just not for me."

Carmindy and thousands of other cosmetologists—rich or not—are doing what they love to do. You can't have a better life than that!

Makeup artists who work in the theatrical industry earn average salaries of nearly $68,000 a year, according to the USDL.

RESEARCH PROJECT

Learn more about the licensing requirements for cosmetologists in your state or country. Write a report that summarizes what you will need to do to become licensed.

TEXT-DEPENDENT QUESTIONS

1. What is involved with an apprenticeship?
2. What is the average salary for cosmetologists?
3. Who is Sally Hershberger?

WORDS TO UNDERSTAND

bookkeeping: keeping track of the money that a business receives and spends

clientele: a group of loyal customers

fundamentals: the basic aspects of something

perseverance: not giving up when faced with a big challenge

CHAPTER 5

KEY SKILLS AND METHODS OF EXPLORATION

WHAT ALL COSMETOLOGISTS NEED

Learning cosmetology skills is only half of what you need in order to become a successful personal appearance worker. You also need certain qualities (distinctive skills or parts of one's personality) that will help you stand out from the crowd and better serve your clients.

The U.S. Department of Labor lists some key qualities for cosmetologists. They must be creative, for example. Customers will come in and ask for a certain hairstyle or makeup. A cosmetologist has to know how to make that happen by picturing it in their head and then doing it. Or the customer might tell a personal appearance worker they want something new, and to do whatever the worker wants. The cosmetologist has to be able to think of a new style and create it on the spot. In a way, cosmetologists are artists who sculpt or paint the human body. They have to have good customer service skills too. Personal appearance professionals work with customers almost all day. They need to be able to talk to them in person, on the phone, via email, and through instant messaging or video chat. Cosmetologists tend to be friendly and open to meeting and talking to new people. Even if they're in a bad mood, they leave it behind them while they work. They always have to be friendly to customers.

Often, cosmetologists love their jobs because they get to talk to so many people. "You have to love serving people, and you have to be patient," says Karen Gordon. "It takes time and **perseverance** to become a great hairdresser and to build a **clientele**, but the rewards are so worth it." She goes on to say, "My clients are the most wonderful people. I have learned so much from them about all sorts of things over the years. They have truly enriched my life."

Time-management skills are another important quality. These include the ability to balance a busy schedule. A hairstylist might see ten customers a day. They always have new and returning customers calling to make appointments. They can't book two appointments at once. Personal appearance workers also often have cleaning and **bookkeeping** to do, so they have to leave themselves breaks in between customers. A cosmetologist with good time-management skills will be able to do all that without a problem.

Karen adds a quality to this list: patience. "A lot of people get frustrated one or two years into the profession because they feel things are not happening fast enough for them," she explains. "It takes time to become really good at hairdressing, and it takes time to build a clientele. Too many people drop out just as they are getting along."

Lots of teenagers experiment with applying each other's makeup. If this is something you love to do, you might consider making a career out of it.

Personal appearance workers need the patience to get better at their trade slowly and to constantly learn new things. A new cosmetologist might also find that it takes a few years to get loyal customers. If they are patient, they'll find customers who will come back again and again. Once that happens, they will truly be successful at their job!

EXPLORING COSMETOLOGY AS A STUDENT

There are many ways to explore a career in cosmetology. And unlike many careers, you can get hands-on experience while you're still in your teens. Here are some suggestions for how to learn more about personal appearance careers.

TRY YOUR HAND AT COSMETOLOGY

If you're thinking about a career in beauty care, you can start practicing and doing some research. Play with makeup, hair, and skin. Practice on your friends, family, and yourself. Try out different things and see what you like best. Read about how to apply makeup, do nails, and cut hair. You can find makeup, hairstyling, and nail care tutorials (lessons) online at YouTube.com and on beauty websites.

TAKE SOME CLASSES

There are many classes that are offered by your high school, community organizations, and beauty schools and associations that can help you prepare for a career in the personal appearance industry. If you attend a vocational or technical school, cosmetology classes will be available. These courses are also offered by local beauty schools. If you're not sure whether a career in cosmetology is for you, take a class or two to explore the field and try out new things. Maybe you'll learn that you'd rather be a skin care specialist or manicurist rather than a hairstylist.

Classes in biology, anatomy, and health will give you a good introduction to the human body and the systems that keep us healthy.

Speech classes will help you to develop your public speaking skills, which you'll use every day on the job.

Taking a foreign language will arm you with the skills to communicate and connect with people from other cultures. This is a good way to increase your client base.

Math classes will be useful when you are coloring or cutting a client's hair. You'll need to have good math skills in order to combine the correct amount of hair coloring to get the desired effect. While they probably don't think about it often, hairstylists use angles, shapes, and math principles when cutting hair. If you plan to own a business, you'll need math skills to manage your finances, to set prices, to establish sales goals, and for many other reasons.

Marketing classes will come in handy whether you're a business owner or a hairstylist who rents a chair at a local salon. You'll need to constantly market yourself to build your client list. You should become an expert at using social media (including Instagram, Twitter, and Facebook) to promote yourself and get people excited about what you do.

A high school student gives a presentation to her class. Developing good communication skills will make it easier to talk with your clients.

Computer classes are useful because many cosmetologists—especially business owners—use databases and other types of software to track appointments, receive payment from customers, manage their finances, and perform other tasks.

TALK TO TEACHERS, COUNSELORS, AND LIBRARIANS

Talk to your guidance counselor at school about becoming a cosmetologist. Your counselor can give you information about different jobs and how to get them. They can point out books and websites you can look at for even more information.

If your high school offers cosmetology courses, talk to the teachers of these classes to get a better understanding of job duties and what it takes to prepare for the field.

Head to your school or local library to get books and videos about hairstyling, skin care, manicuring, and other cosmetology specialties.

PARTICIPATE IN A COMPETITION

Competing in a hairstyling or other type of cosmetology contest is a good way to develop and test your skills. It's also a great way to build your personal and professional network (a group of people you know who can help you get a job or meet other life goals) and make some lifelong friends. International, national, or regional associations, schools, businesses, and other organizations sponsor competitions. Here are two competitions to check out:

Participating in a makeup competition is a great way to test your creative skills against those of others.

SkillsUSA

SkillsUSA is a national membership organization for middle school, high school, and college students who are preparing for careers in technical, trade, and skilled service occupations. It offers a Cosmetology competition in which students demonstrate their skills in haircutting, hair styling, and long-hair design in four separate tests. There is also an Esthetics competition in which contestants take a written knowledge exam that covers the **fundamentals** of skin care, give a professional oral presentation, and participate in four hands-on technical skill performance tasks that consist of a facial cleansing massage, basic facial, beauty makeup, and fantasy makeup applications. A Nail Care contest is also available. SkillsUSA works directly with high schools and colleges, so ask your school counselor or teacher if it is an option for you. Learn more at www.skillsusa.org.

Skills Compétences Canada

Skills Compétences Canada is a nonprofit organization that seeks to encourage Canadian youth to pursue careers in the skilled trades and technology sectors.

Its National Competition allows young people to participate in more than forty skilled trade and technology competitions, including Hairstyling and Aesthetics. For the Hairstyling competition, participants will be asked to perform the following cuts on a mannequin: men's fashion cut and style, bridal long-hair up, ladies fashion haircut, and men's modern classic haircut and style. During the Aesthetics contest, participants will demonstrate the techniques that are involved in an advanced facial, a manicure with nail art, a body therapy treatment with hair removal, and a

SOURCES OF ADDITIONAL EXPLORATION

Contact the following organizations for more information on education and careers in cosmetology:

American Association of Cosmetology Schools
www.beautyschools.org

Hair and Beauty Industry Association
https://hbia.com.au

International Spa Association
https://experienceispa.com

National Accrediting Commission of Career Arts and Sciences
www.naccas.org

Professional Beauty Association
https://probeauty.org

Spa Industry Association
www.dayspaassociation.com

Get a behind-the-scenes look at the Style Masters Hair Competition.

creative makeup presentation. Learn more at http://skillscompetencescanada.com/en/skills-canada-national-competition.

CONDUCT AN INFORMATION INTERVIEW WITH A COSMETOLOGIST

Talk to cosmetologists too—they're the best sources of information. When you get your hair cut, for example, ask your hairstylist lots of questions and find out how they got their job. The more people you talk to, the better you'll understand what cosmetology is like. You might even want to turn this informal talk into an information interview.

An information interview simply involves talking with a personal appearance worker about their educational background, work environment, job duties, and other topics that will help you decide if this is a good career for you. Many information interviews are conducted in person, but you can also conduct such an interview on the phone and via email or online video chat. Here are some questions to ask during the interview:

- Can you tell me about a day in your life on the job?
- Is your job physically demanding? If so, what do you do to keep yourself healthy on the job?
- What type of equipment do you use on the job?
- What are the most important personal and professional qualities for cosmetologists? Business owners?
- How do you use technology in your work?
- What do you do when you have a challenging customer?
- What do you like best and least about your job?
- What is the future employment outlook for cosmetologists? How is the field changing?
- What can I do now to prepare for the field?
- Can you tell me about the licensing process? What did you have to do to become licensed? Was the process challenging?
- If you could go back in time, would you become a cosmetologist again?

JOB SHADOW A COSMETOLOGIST

In a job shadowing experience, which is always done in person, you watch personal appearance workers on the job. You'll observe them as they cut and style a client's hair, give manicures, apply skin care treatments, and perform other tasks. You can also see how they interact with customers, and what it takes to run a business. Job shadowing experiences also provide an excellent opportunity to ask cosmetologists questions about their work.

Visiting a hair salon and observing hairstylists is an excellent way to learn more about the field.

RESEARCH PROJECT

Learn as much as you can about hairstyling. Perhaps your hairstylist can give you a few basic tips and let you watch them on the job. What skills discussed in this chapter were used by the hairstylist? Write a report that summarizes how they were used and present it to your class.

TEXT-DEPENDENT QUESTIONS

1. Why do personal appearance workers need good customer service skills?
2. Why are good time-management skills important for cosmetologists?
3. What are three ways to explore the field of cosmetology?

WORDS TO UNDERSTAND

disposable income: money that is available after living expenses (rent, food, etc.) are paid

economy: activities related to production, consumption, and trade of services and goods in a city, state, region, or country

luxury: something that is not necessary but sends a message of wealth and success

networking: the process of connecting with people by talking about shared experiences and interests; networking leads to new work opportunities

CHAPTER 6

LOOKING TO THE FUTURE

GROWING OPPORTUNITIES FOR PERSONAL APPEARANCE WORKERS

The future looks bright for personal appearance workers and for young people who are interested in entering the field. The following sections provide more information on the employment outlook for several beauty care specialties.

HAIRSTYLISTS AND BARBERS

Employment for hairstylists and barbers will grow by 13 percent through 2026, according to the U.S. Department of Labor. This growth is faster than the average growth for all careers. Tens of thousands more hairstylists and barbers will be hired over the next five or so years. Personal appearance—especially the look of one's hair—is very important regardless of where one lives in the world. People will always want to look beautiful, which suggests that there will always be demand for hairstylists and barbers.

There will continue to be good opportunities for barbers as older barbers continue to retire in large numbers.

Over the next few years, plenty of hairstylists and barbers will retire. Or they will get different jobs or start working part time instead of full time. When all these workers leave, new hairstylists and barbers will have the chance to start their careers. Salons might even expand as more customers come to them. Those salons will hire additional hairstylists and barbers to work with all the new customers.

Hairstylists will find that getting a job at a fancy salon where the pay is better won't be as easy. High-end salons only take the best hairstylists who have the most experience. If your goal is to work in one of these salons, it's a good idea to get as much work experience as you can before you start applying. Only the people who work the hardest and have excellent **networking** skills will end up with these jobs.

MANICURISTS AND PEDICURISTS

Employment for manicurists and pedicurists is also expected to grow by 13 percent through 2026, according to the USDL. Job opportunities are increasing for several reasons. First, demand for new types of nail services, such as mini-sessions (quick manicures at a low cost) and mobile manicures and pedicures (nail services that are offered outside of the salon), is fueling the need for these workers. Manicures and pedicures are considered a low-cost **luxury** service, which makes them affordable and desired by individuals at all income levels. Finally, more manicurists and pedicurists will be needed to replace those who retire or leave the field for other reasons.

SKIN CARE SPECIALISTS

Job opportunities for skin care specialists are expected to grow by 14 percent, according to the USDL. Demand for mini-sessions and mobile facials and society's continuing desire to look younger via healthier skin will fuel demand for skin care specialists.

FACTORS THAT MAY SLOW GROWTH

The demand for beauty services will never go away, but a few developments may slow growth for cosmetologists.

Job growth has been good lately, but if the **economy** becomes weak, people will have less **disposable income** to spend on haircuts, manicures, skin care treatments, and other personal care services. Customers may put off getting their hair cut or colored as often as they did when the economy was strong. They may also decide to save money by doing their own beauty treatments at home to save money. When the economy is weak, there will be fewer opportunities for cosmetologists, and they will have to work harder to make a living.

It may also be harder to get a job if the number of people training for the field increases. To prepare for potential competition, it's a good idea to learn as many personal care skills (hair styling, makeup, skin care, massage, etc.) as possible to appeal to a wider clientele.

DESAIROLOGY

Desairology is not for everyone, but it can be an adventure for the right person. A desairologist works with the hair of dead people to make them look peaceful and beautiful for funerals. They may also apply makeup and work on the decedent's nails. Desairologists help make funerals and death a little easier for loved ones. Most desairologists don't work full time. They may also work with living people, or have another job entirely the rest of the time.

Finally, the growing use of robots in a variety of work settings may eventually limit job opportunities for people in many professions, including cosmetology. A few years back, Panasonic created a prototype for a robot hair washer that uses advanced robot "fingers" to massage the scalp while washing one's hair, but it is not in everyday use. Many believe that it will be a long time before robots can replace cosmetologists. Each person's hair, nails, skin type, and other physical qualities are unique, which would make it hard for a robot to be able to master a haircut, manicure, or skin care treatment. Additionally, many people enjoy the interaction they have with their hairstylist and wouldn't want to trade this experience for one with a scissor-wielding robot.

IN CLOSING

Are you fascinated by new hairstyles, makeup, and skin care treatments? Do you like making others more beautiful? Do you have good hand-eye coordination and excellent communication and people skills? Are you creative, and do you like learning new things? If so, a career as a cosmetologist might be in your future. Use this book and other resources to continue to explore your interest in a career in beauty care. Good luck with your career exploration!

There are many great career paths—including manicurist—in the cosmetology industry.

RESEARCH PROJECT

Interview three cosmetologists about the future of the career. Ask them how technology and other developments will change the field. Write a report that summarizes your findings and present it to your class.

TEXT-DEPENDENT QUESTIONS

1. Why is the employment outlook good for cosmetologists?
2. What factors could cause job growth to slow?
3. What is desairology?

SERIES GLOSSARY
OF KEY TERMS

accreditation: The process of being evaluated and approved by a governing body as providing excellent coursework, products, or services. Quality college and university educational programs are accredited.

application materials: Items, such as a cover letter, resume, and letters of recommendation, that one provides to employers when applying for a job or an internship.

apprenticeship: A formal training program that combines classroom instruction and supervised practical experience. Apprentices are paid a salary that increases as they obtain experience.

associate's degree: A degree that requires a two-year course of study after high school.

bachelor's degree: A degree that requires a four-year course of study after high school.

certificate: A credential that shows a person has completed specialized education, passed a test, and met other requirements to qualify for work in a career or industry. College certificate programs typically last six months to a year.

certification: A credential that one earns by passing a test and meeting other requirements. Certified workers have a better chance of landing a job than those who are not certified. They also often earn higher salaries than those who are not certified.

community college: A private or public two-year college that awards certificates and associates degrees.

consultant: An experienced professional who is self-employed and provides expertise about a particular subject.

cover letter: A one-page letter in which a job seeker summarizes their educational and professional background, skills, and achievements, as well as states their interest in a job.

doctoral degree: A degree that is awarded to an individual who completes two or three additional years of education after earning a master's degree. It is also known as a doctorate.

for-profit business: One that seeks to earn money for its owners.

fringe benefits: A payment or non-financial benefit that is given to a worker in addition to salary. These consist of cash bonuses for good work, paid vacations and sick days, and health and life insurance.

information interview: The process of interviewing a person about their career, whether in person, by phone, online, or by email.

internship: A paid or unpaid learning opportunity in which a student works at a business to obtain experience for anywhere from a few weeks to a year.

job interview: A phone, internet, or in-person meeting in which a job applicant presents their credentials to a hiring manager.

job shadowing: The process of following a worker around while they do their job, with the goal of learning more about a particular career and building one's network.

licensing: Official permission that is granted by a government agency to a person in a particular field (nursing, engineering, etc.) to practice in their profession. Licensing requirements typically involve meeting educational and experience requirements, and sometimes passing a test.

master's degree: A two-year, graduate-level degree that is earned after a student first completes a four-year bachelor's degree.

mentor: An experienced professional who provides advice to a student or inexperienced worker (mentee) regarding personal and career development.

minimum wage: The minimum amount that a worker can be paid by law.

nonprofit organization: A group that uses any profits it generates to advance its stated goals (protecting the environment, helping the homeless, etc.). It is not a corporation or other for-profit business.

professional association: An organization that is founded by a group of people who have the same career (engineers, professional hackers, scientists, etc.) or who work in the same industry (information technology, health care, etc.).

professional network: Friends, family, coworkers, former teachers, and others who can help you find a job.

recruiting firm: A company that matches job seekers with job openings.

registered apprenticeship: A program that meets standards of fairness, safety, and training established by the U.S. government or local governments.

resume: A formal summary of one's educational and work experience that is submitted to a potential employer.

salary: Money one receives for doing work.

scholarship: Money that is awarded to students to pay for college and other types of education; it does not have to be paid back.

self-employed: Working for oneself as a small business owner, rather than for a corporation or other employer. Self-employed people must generate their own income and provide their own fringe benefits (such as health insurance).

soft skills: Personal abilities that people need to develop to be successful on the job—communication, work ethic, teamwork, decision-making, positivity, time management, flexibility, problem-solving, critical thinking, conflict resolution, and other skills and traits.

technical college: A public or private college that offers two- or four-year programs in practical subjects, such as the trades, information technology, applied sciences, agriculture, and engineering.

union: An organization that seeks to gain better wages, benefits, and working conditions for its members. Also called a **labor union** or **trade union**.

work-life balance: A healthy balance of time spent on the job and time spent with family and on leisure activities.

FURTHER READING & INTERNET RESOURCES

FURTHER READING

Hernandez, Gabriela. *Classic Beauty: The History of Makeup*. 2nd ed. Atglen, PA: Schiffer Publishing, 2017.

Milady. *Milady's Standard Cosmetology*. 13th ed. Independence, KY: Milady, 2015.

Sunnydale, Helena. *The Complete Book of Beauty: The Ultimate Guide To Skincare, Makeup, Haircare, Hairstyling, Diet, and Fitness*. Cambridgeshire, U.K.: Lorenz Books, 2016.

Young, Louise, and Loulia Sheppard. *Timeless: Recreate the Classic Makeup and Hairstyles from 100 Years of Beauty*. Philadelphia: Running Press, 2018.

INTERNET RESOURCES

www.bls.gov/ooh/personal-care-and-service/barbers-hairstylists-and-cosmetologists.htm: This section of the *Occupational Outlook Handbook* features information on job duties, educational requirements, salaries, and the employment outlook for barbers, hairstylists, and cosmetologists.

https://beautychangeslives.org: Beauty Changes Lives offers information on cosmetology careers and scholarships.

www.bls.gov/ooh/personal-care-and-service/skincare-specialists.htm: This section of the *Occupational Outlook Handbook* provides information on job responsibilities, potential educational paths, key skills, earnings, and the employment outlook for skin care specialists.

https://beautisecrets.com/history-of-cosmetology: This website provides a history of cosmetology—from ancient Mesopotamia to the present day.

www.behindthechair.com: Visit this website for hair styling tips and techniques and other useful resources.

EDUCATIONAL VIDEO LINKS

Chapter 1
Learn more about education and careers in cosmetology:
http://x-qr.net/1JgP

Chapter 2
A hair salon owner discusses why she entered the field and the rewards and challenges of her work:
http://x-qr.net/1Hut

Chapter 4
Learn about a cosmetology training program for high school students: http://x-qr.net/1LrG

Learn five things you should consider before enrolling in a beauty school: http://x-qr.net/1Lqs

Chapter 5
Get a behind-the-scenes look at the Style Masters Hair Competition: http://x-qr.net/1HuY

INDEX

AUTHOR BIOGRAPHIES

Andrew Morkes has been a writer and editor for more than twenty-five years. He is the author of more than twenty-five books about college planning and careers, including all of the titles in this series, many titles in the Careers in the Building Trades series, the *Vault Career Guide to Social Media*, and *They Teach That in College!?: A Resource Guide to More Than 100 Interesting College Majors*, which was selected as one of the best books of the year by the library journal *Voice of Youth Advocates*. He is also the author and publisher of "The Morkes Report: College and Career Planning Trends" blog.

Christie Marlowe lives in Binghamton, New York, where she works as a writer and web designer. She has a degree in literature, cares strongly about the environment, and spends three or more nights a week wailing on her Telecaster.

PHOTO CREDITS